The Wonderful World of Colour

COLOUR IN COMMUNICATION

SALLY AND ADRIAN MORGAN

Evans

Published by Evans Brothers Limited
2A Portman Mansions
Chiltern Street
London W1M 1LE

© copyright in the text and illustrations
Evans Brothers Limited 1993

First published in 1993

Printed in Hong Kong

ISBN 0 237 51274 2

Acknowledgments

Editorial: Catherine Chambers and Jean Coppendale
Design: Monica Chia
Illustrations: Hardlines, Charlbury
Production: Peter Thompson

For permission to reproduce copyright material the author and publishers gratefully acknowledge the following:
Cover: Main photograph – International Flags – Thomas Buchholz, Bruce Coleman Limited; inset photograph – A traditional Chinese wedding – The Hutchison Library
Title page: Olympic flag – Grafton M Smith, The Image Bank
Contents page: Indian Chief – Stephen Marks, The Image Bank
Page 6 – (above) Ecoscene, (below) Jones, Ecoscene; page 7 – (top) John Downman, The Hutchison Library, (middle) Simon Fraser, Science Photo Library, (bottom) Zefa Picture Library (UK) Ltd; page 8 – (top) Sally Morgan, Ecoscene, (middle) Towse, Ecoscene, (bottom) Derek Redfearn, The Image Bank; page 9 – (main picture) Romilly Lockyer, The Image Bank, (top) Eric Meola, The Image Bank, (middle) Platt, Ecoscene, (bottom) Sally Morgan, Ecoscene; page 10 – (top) Trip, Eye Ubiquitous, (bottom left) Tony Craddock, Science Photo Library, (right) Thomas Buchholz, Bruce Coleman Limited; page 11 – Sally Morgan, Ecoscene; page 12 – Sally Morgan, Ecoscene; page 13 – (left) Adam Woolfitt, Robert Harding Picture Library, (top right) S Achernar, The Image Bank, (bottom right) Greenwood, Ecoscene; page 14 – (left) Patti McConville, The Image Bank, (right) Don Lester, Ecoscene, page 15 – Sally Morgan, Ecoscene; page 16 – Groves, Ecoscene; page 17 – (top) Anthony King, (bottom) R Issing, Zentrale Farbbild Agentur GmbH; page 19 – (top) MacIntyre, The Hutchison Library, (bottom) Robert Harding Picture Library; page 20 – (left) Sally Morgan, Ecoscene, (right) Peter Miller, The Image Bank; page 21 – Helene Rogers, Trip; page 22 – (top left) Himmat Kalsia, (top right) Harwood, Ecoscene, (bottom) Lars Ternblad, The Image Bank; page 24 – Norman Myers, Bruce Coleman Ltd; page 25 – (left) Platt, Ecoscene, (right) Melanie Friend, The Hutchison Library; page 26 – (top left) Emma Lee, Life File, (top right) Robert Harding Picture Library, (bottom) Jones, Ecoscene; page 27 – Robert Harding Picture Library; page 28 – (top) STB/Still Moving Picture Company, (bottom) Harwood, Ecoscene; page 30 – (top) Robert Harding Picture Library, (bottom) Walter Rawlings, Robert Harding Picture Library; page 31 – (left) Stephen Marks, The Image Bank, (right) Ecoscene; page 32 – (top) 'Cecil', Jean Coppendale, (bottom) Robert Harding Picture Library; page 33 – A C Waltham, Robert Harding Picture Library; page 34 – (top) Christopher Rennie, Robert Harding Picture Library, (bottom) Cooper, Ecoscene; page 35 – (left) Kloske, Ecoscene, (right) Peter Hewson, Trip, Eye Ubiquitous; page 36 – (left) Robert Harding Picture Library, (right) The Hutchison Library; page 37 – (top) Jones, Ecoscene, (bottom) Trip; page 38 – Juliet Highet, Life File; page 39 – (top) J H C Wilson, Robert Harding Picture Library, (bottom) The Hutchison Library; page 40 – (top) Stephen Marks, The Image Bank, (bottom) Robert Cundy, Robert Harding Picture Library; page 41 – (left) Helene Rogers, Trip, (right) Robert Harding Picture Library; page 42 – (top) G M Wilkins, Robert Harding Picture Library, (bottom) Trevor Page, The Hutchison Library; page 43 (left) The Hutchison Library, (right) Liba Taylor, The Hutchison Library; page 44 – Associated Press/Topham; page 45 – G Hellier, Robert Harding Picture Library

Contents

The meanings of the words in bold can be found in the COLOURFUL WORDS! boxes throughout the book.

Introduction

The light from the Sun is often called white light. However, sunlight is not a single colour but a mixture of many colours. Our eyes can see seven of these colours: red, orange, yellow, green, blue, indigo and violet. Together, they form a spectrum. The colours in a rainbow, which only appears where there is rain and sunlight, are those of a spectrum. They form because 'white' sunlight is bent as it passes through each raindrop. The colours in sunlight are each bent by different amounts, so the light is split up into beams of different colours. These form a rainbow. Blue light is bent more than red light, so blue is seen on one side and red on the other.

Above: Bright face painting on a Huli tribesman from Papua New Guinea
Below: Multicoloured tri-shaws, or *becaks* for hire in Java, Indonesia

A spectrum also forms when white light is passed through a special piece of glass called a prism. Ultra-violet and Infrared are colours of light at either end of the spectrum. But we cannot see them; they are invisible to our eyes, although some animals can detect them. Ultra-violet light causes white skin to turn brown in the Sun, and can harm our eyes. Infrared light is given off by all living organisms, and can be seen by special cameras that are sensitive to this light. Infra-red light is often used in TV remote controls.

There are two special cells in our eyes that are sensitive to light. They are called rods and cones. The rods provide us with black and white vision. They are quite sensitive to any light, however faint it is, so they help us to see at night. But they cannot detect colours. Cones, on the other hand, can detect light of different colours. But because they are less sensitive, they are not much use at night when it is dark.

Not all animals can see in colour. Dogs, for example, cannot see all the colours that we see. Their world is mostly shades of black, white and grey. However, insects such as the honey-bee can see Ultra-violet light, a colour that our eyes cannot detect.

In this book we are going to find out how we use colour to communicate warnings, instructions, ideas and feelings. We live in a colourful world, so colour is a very important

feature of our everyday lives. We see a red traffic light, and we stop, because we know it means danger. The particular colours of a football shirt show to which team a player belongs. We get a huge amount of information from colour; much more than we could possibly get if we could only see in black and white.

Impfgebiet
TOLLWUT

In diesem Gebiet sind z. Z.
Impfköder mit Tollwut-Impfstoff so ausgelegt,
daß Füchse sie aufnehmen und damit gegen Tollwut
geschützt werden.

Bitte beachten:
• Impfköder nicht berühren   • Bei Kontakt Arzt oder Tierarzt
• Hunde nicht frei laufen lassen   befragen
• Haustiere von Impfködern   • Informieren Sie bitte Ihre Kinder
  fernhalten

Landratsamt

Top: International flags and Amsterdam's yellow trams
Above: A bright danger sign warning that food with rabies vaccine in it has been laid down for foxes to eat

Left: Almost every Muslim pilgrim is dressed in white in Mecca as a sign of purity

Colours for information

Colours on signs

Colour helps to make information clear, and quick to understand. It is therefore very important in the design of road signs, timetables, maps and brochures.

Road signs use colour and shape to give warnings and information. Strangers in large cities need street signs that give them information quickly. So colours and shapes have to be clear, to give a simple message.

Throughout most of Europe, signs on motorways and those directing drivers to them have a blue background. On main roads, the background is green. On smaller roads, such as country lanes, a white background is used. Signs showing places of interest are normally brown and sometimes have special symbols, such as a castle. Holiday routes are marked with a yellow diamond shape, while diversions are usually indicated on a yellow sign. Many cities around the world now use the same symbols to show people where tourist information centres, museums and hospitals can be found.

For a visitor, colours are very important for maps and guides. In cities different routes for buses and underground trains are often given a particular colour. This is called colour coding. Museums, zoos and even large exhibitions and fairs use a similar system. In popular mountain resorts

White signs on a minor road in France

This town has many tourist attractions, including a museum. What do you think the different symbols mean?

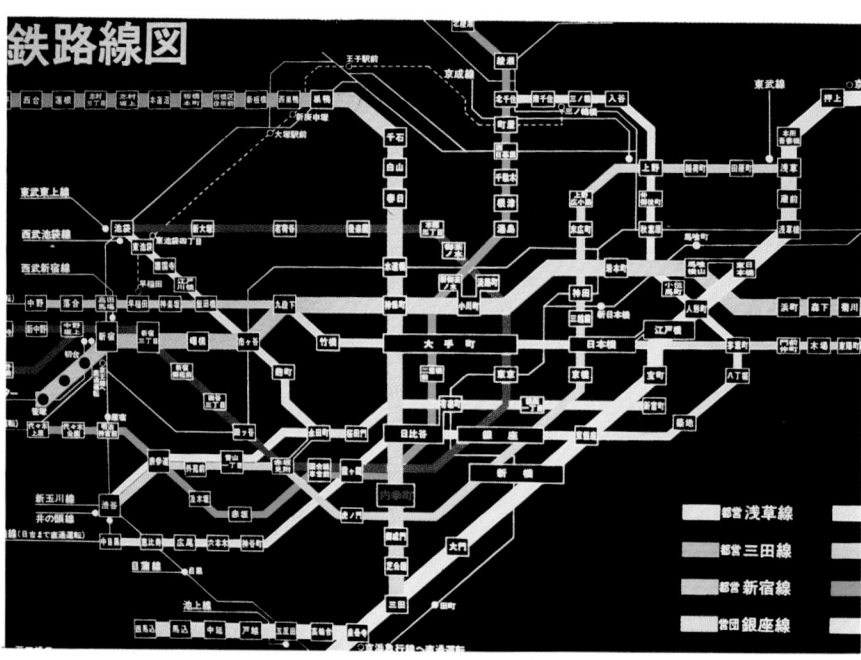

An underground map in Tokyo, Japan, shows many different routes. Each one has been colour coded

and national parks, nature trails and walks are often colour coded so that people do not get lost.

Large coloured symbols are used to mark out ski slopes so that skiers know if a slope is easy or difficult to ski down. Easy slopes are marked blue, those of medium difficulty are marked red, and black markers show difficult slopes. The markers are also numbered, and ski maps of the area use the same colours and numbers that are on the markers.

The same system is used for water rides in some of the very large water parks.

Colours for safety

Most of our road safety signs use bold colours and simple shapes. Drivers need to spot a sign easily and instantly understand what it means.

In most countries, a road sign in the shape of a triangle is a warning of a danger ahead: perhaps a hill, a narrow road, a bridge, animals on the road, or roadworks. A circular sign, though, gives an order, such as STOP! Information signs are usually square. They give directions or tell people where they are allowed to park their vehicles. In North America, there are diamond-shaped signs, and even hexagonal ones. Although signs are made in these different shapes, it would be much harder for motorists if every sign was only in black and white.

Roads would be very dangerous without traffic lights. The same colours are used in traffic lights throughout the world, so everybody knows what they mean, even if they do not know the local language. Red and green lights are also used

A sign marking a ski slope

A sign warning drivers that kangaroos might cross the road in front of them

A tractor warning sign on a road in California

Icy road, snow and low cloud warnings on a mountain road in Italy

COLOURFUL THINGS TO DO!

Spotting the signs
Next time you visit your local town, have a good look at road signs and markings. You will need a notebook and pencil. Draw some of the signs that you see. Make a note of their colour. Can you put the signs into different groups? What types of sign are yellow? Which ones are blue, and which have a red triangle? If you are not sure what a sign means you can always look it up in the Highway Code. If you ride a bike, it is very important to know what different road signs mean.

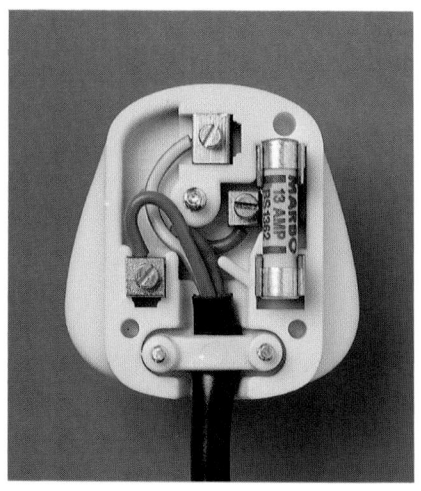

This plug has been properly wired with three plastic covered wires. The brown wire is known as the 'live' wire, the blue wire is 'neutral' and the yellow and green is the 'earth'

on railways to tell train drivers when to stop and when to go. In Venice, traffic lights are used to control boat movements on the many canals.

Electrical appliances, such as kettles and irons, have to be connected safely to a plug. This is done by using a system of coloured wires. When the plug is put into a socket, electricity can flow from the main electricity supply along a cable. The cable has the same system of coloured wires as the plug. In many countries there are three wires inside electricity cables; some countries have just two. When three wires are used, they are covered in brown, blue, and green and yellow plastic so that it is easy to tell the difference between each one. The plug can then be wired up safely.

Warning colours

Special colours are often used to warn people of danger. Emergency vehicles have to travel very fast when they are needed. So bright red fire-engines are easy to spot in the day time. White is one of the best colours for vehicles as it can be seen at night. Ambulances and police cars are often white. Many have an orange fluorescent strip around them, and flashing coloured lights on the roofs.

Yellow is an easy colour to see because our eyes are particularly sensitive to yellow and can detect it even in dim light. For this reason, it is a very effective warning colour, and is used for marking lines on roads. It is also used with black to warn people about moving parts of machinery, or the danger of **radiation**. Even in nature, yellow gives a warning signal. The black and yellow stripes of a wasp

Above: A symbol warning of the danger of radiation
Right: Fire-engines in Kiel, Germany

A warning bar near dangerous paper making machinery stops workers from going too close when the machines are running

show that it can sting. The yellow markings of certain poisonous snakes and frogs are reminders that the animal is dangerous, or unpleasant to eat.

All around the world chemicals are being transported and stored. In schools, hospitals and factories there are often stores of chemicals. It is important that people who come into contact with them know how dangerous they can be. For a long time different countries had different symbols for chemicals, but this was not very helpful if the chemical was transported to other parts of the world. In Europe there is now an agreement on the colour and symbol that should be used for each chemical. Some of these symbols are shown below. The symbols are easy to understand but sometimes words are added to make sure there is no confusion. If you look carefully at the back of a tanker that is carrying chemicals or other dangerous substances, you will see a panel. This is covered in information which tells people what is inside the tanker, and how to deal with the chemical if it is spilt.

Explosive chemicals

Inflammable chemicals

Harmful chemicals

Poisonous chemicals

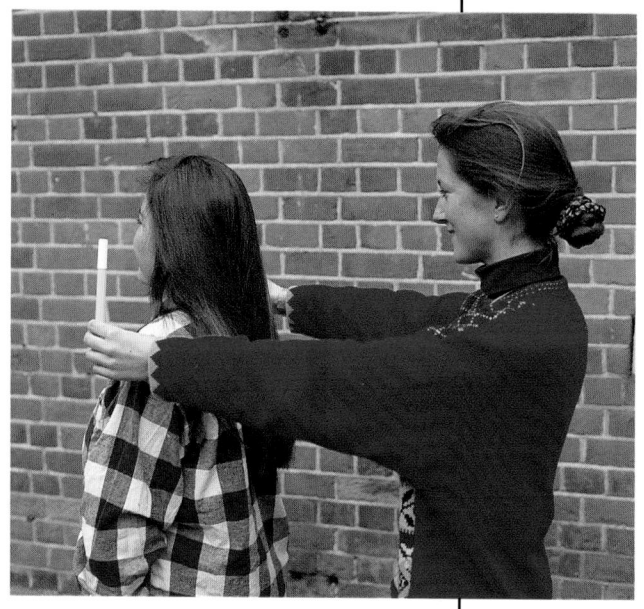

COLOURFUL THINGS TO DO!

Warning colours

Emergency vehicles, such as fire-engines, are brightly coloured. These colours are easy to spot, and we are aware of them even out of the corner of our eye. In this project you will discover which colours are easiest to see out of the corner of your eye. You will need a friend to help you, and a selection of brightly-coloured felt-tip pens. The casing of each pen must be brightly coloured, not just the ink inside.

1 Get a friend to stand or sit with their back towards you.

2 Take two pens, each a different colour.

3 Hold one pen in each of your hands, and hold your arms out at either side of your friend, level with their ears.

4 Get your friend to look straight ahead, and ask them if they can see either of the pens out the corner of their eye.

5 If they cannot see either pen, move the pens together slightly forward until they can just see one or the other. Which pen colour is spotted first? Do this again, but with different coloured pens, and find out which colours can be seen quickly.

Colour in facts and figures

Colours are very important in presenting facts and figures for reports and books. They make information clearer. Students can understand new information more easily, and business people at a conference can grasp it very quickly. Line graphs, bar graphs and pie charts can be drawn in different colours to make each part stand out more clearly.

COLOURFUL THINGS TO DO!

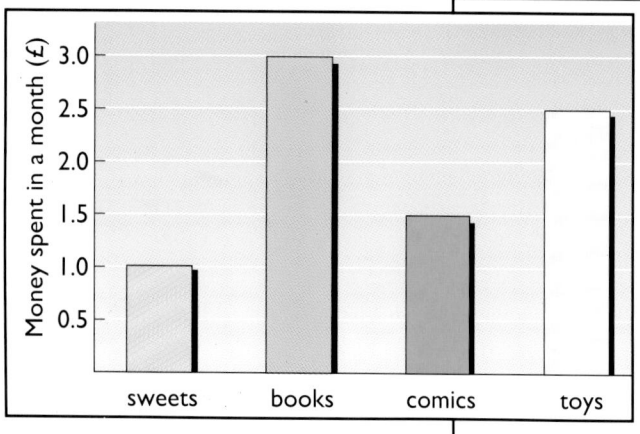

You might want to show how much of your pocket money has been spent on, say, comics, sweets, books and toys over a certain length of time. You could draw a bar graph like the one in the diagram. The figures going up the left-hand side show the number of pounds spent. Each bar is short or long depending on the amount of money given for each item. Colour in each section using a different colour. It is now easy to see if too much of your money has been spent on sweets!

Colours on maps

A map can tell you a great deal about an area. Colour is used to help the reader understand the information given on a map. Even if you did not know much about maps, you could quickly look at one and see that rivers, lakes and the sea are coloured blue. The areas that are covered by

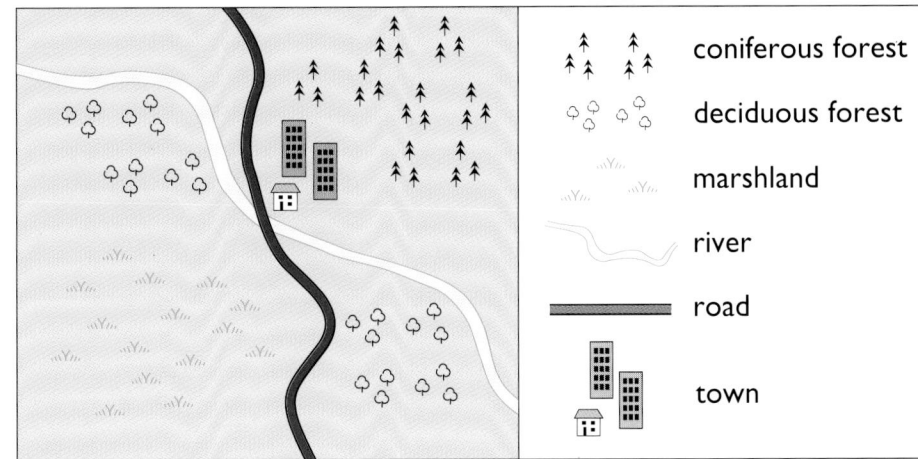

woodland or forest are green. They have symbols to show the type of forest, that is, whether the trees in it are **deciduous** or **coniferous**.

The roads on maps are also coloured. In the UK, motorways are blue, main 'A' roads are red, 'B' class roads are brown, and small roads and tracks are yellow or white. Footpaths and bridle paths are also marked, using a red dotted line. In many other European countries, such as France and Spain, the main routes are marked in red and the 'B' roads are green. Some road maps in the USA mark main roads with thin red lines, and toll roads with a thick red line. Other important roads are black.

In hilly areas it is important to know how high the land is. So some maps, including the types used by tourists, use a series of colours to show the height of the land above sea level. Land up to 200 metres above sea level is very pale green, between 200 and 400 metres the land is shaded in yellow, and above 400 the land is given shades of brown. The highest land is the darkest brown.

These coloured maps give a very good idea of the type of landscape in an area. They help people to plan their visit

Look at the three pictures below. Can you see how the marshland and the two types of forest have been shown on the map?

Top right: Coniferous forest
Above: Marshland
Left: Deciduous forest

13

and perhaps work out routes for walking. It is easy to see where there are buildings, because the built-up areas, such as housing estates or factory sites, are marked in a pale brown.

Symbols are often used with colour to make particular points of interest easy to spot. A church can be marked as a black cross. There is often a square attached to the cross if the church has a tower, or a circle if the church has a spire. Car parks, places of interest and nature reserves are also marked in different colours.

In an atlas, the maps give us more information about the world and the countries in it. Seas are shown in blue, with the deeper areas of the sea being shown in darker shades of blue. Rainfall, temperature, and hours of sunlight can all be shown on a map by colour **scales**. They can be similar to the one used to show the height of land. Rainfall maps often have red and yellow to show drier areas. Wet areas have shades of blue that get increasingly darker where rainfall becomes heavier. Maps showing temperature use 'hot' colours such as yellow and red for hot regions. Cooler parts of the world are shown in green and blue. Some maps show us the different types of **habitat** around the world,

Right: A church with a steeple and its symbol

 *Below:* A church with a spire and its symbol

such as rainforest. Each habitat is given a different colour, so the reader can easily get an idea where the habitats can be found.

How would you show this river-gorge, the hills and the deciduous woodland on a map?

COLOURFUL THINGS TO DO!

Map your local area

You can easily produce a map of your local area - perhaps your own street, school or even your own home and garden. You could make a map of the room you are sitting in right now. All you will need are some colouring crayons, pencils, a notebook and a large piece of white paper.

1 Walk around the area that you are going to map. Make a note of the points of interest. For example, is there a church, post office, shops or school? What types of road pass through the area?

2 Go home and start to draw out the map using your pencil first.

3 When you are sure that you have all the roads in the right place, start to use colours to make them show up. Remember to use bright colours that are easy to spot.

4 You will have to draw a key in the corner of the map. A key tells the reader what all the different colours and symbols mean.

COLOURFUL WORDS!

radiation: high-energy particles that are sent out into the air

coniferous: trees such as the pine, which have cones to hold the seeds, and needle-like leaves which stay green all year round

deciduous: trees that lose their leaves in winter, such as the oak

scale: the relation between a length on a map and the real distance on the ground

habitat: the natural home of a plant or animal

Colours for status

Colour has often been used to show status, or people's position in society. Sometimes it shows what jobs they do. Manual workers, or people who work with their hands, are sometimes called 'blue collar' workers. Managers, and people who work in offices, are called 'white collar' workers. This is because of the colour of the work clothes which people used to wear. Manual workers' overalls were often made from heavy blue cotton, while managers and office workers wore a suit with a white shirt and collar.

In Roman times, the colour of a man's **toga** showed his status. A Senator's toga was edged with purple, while an Emperor's was purple all over. Purple **dye** was very expensive, so dying your clothes purple was a sign of wealth.

In some countries, though, colour has been used to make people look the same. In communist China the entire population used to wear the same colour clothes, a denim blue, to show that everyone should be treated in the same way (see pages 32-33). The word 'communism' means that the wealth of a country should be shared by all the people. Today there are changes in China. People have more freedom and not everybody wears blue.

Men in blue sitting outside an electrical shop in Peking, China

Among the Hausa people in northern Nigeria and southern Niger, the local rulers, or *sarkuna,* wear white turbans. Their palace officials wear shiny, deep blue ones. The material used for the turbans is dipped into dye pits filled with a dark blue liquid made from the leaves of indigo plants. A beautiful shine is made by beating the dyed cloth. There are other members of the palace staff who can be identified by their coloured turbans. Court musicians wear multicoloured ones to draw attention to themselves. The musicians criticize the *sarkuna* in their songs. But the *sarkuna* cannot avoid the singers with their bright turbans!

A Hausa palace official on horseback with his indigo blue turban

White feathers with black tips come from eagles such as the Bald Eagle. North American Indians believe that this magnificent bird was the master of the skies. The feathers are worn as badges of achievement, and so are signs of power or importance. The tail feathers of the eagle used to be prized possessions and were very valuable. Just 24 tail feathers were enough to buy a good horse. The Indians did not kill eagles to collect their feathers. Instead, they either trapped the adult birds and kept them in captivity or they took young birds from the nest and raised them. The feathers were worn in the hair or as part of a war cap. Some were hung on the mane of a favourite horse, or were attached to a sacred smoking pipe (see page 31).

Colour in competition

Players of judo and other similar sports wear a loose-fitting white robe with a belt around the waist. The colour of the belt shows the level of their ability. Beginners wear a white belt. As a person becomes more skilled they progress to yellow, then green and so on, up to black. A very few people who are highly skilled may be awarded the rare red belt. So it is very easy to work out how good somebody is at these sports by simply looking at the colour of their belt.

In many sports competitions, gold, silver and bronze medals are awarded to contestants. The value of the metal from which the medal is made indicates the status and importance of the award. Gold is a more valuable metal than silver or bronze. This is why a gold medal is awarded to the competitor who comes first.

COLOURFUL WORDS!

toga: a loose-fitting robe worn by men in ancient Rome

dye: a colouring usually used on fabrics

Black belt and yellow belt tai kwondo players

Colourful flags

What is a flag? This may seem a very simple question, for we see flags almost every day, blowing in the wind. But flags can be used to communicate many different messages. They are usually made from a piece of fabric, or cloth, which is attached to a pole, often by a rope. Most flags are rectangular, but they can come in many other shapes such as squares, triangles, or even diamonds. The design and colour of flags mean something to the people who look at them, and to their owners.

Why are flags used? Flags are frequently used to represent a particular group or to pass on a message, although nowadays they are also commonly used for decoration. They are used to identify a person, a king or queen, or a country. Flags can show **allegiance**, membership, or loyalty to a particular group or club.

The first flags

Flags have been used for thousands of years. In the past, they were made in more complicated shapes than those seen today, for they were used much more. So it was important to make them as different from each other as possible. Sometimes they were not made from a fabric. The very earliest flags were poles with a carved shape at the top. The ancient Egyptians had fan-shaped flags carved from solid wood, on top of long wooden poles. North American Indians used to make their flags by strapping feathers to the ends of poles.

The Roman **legions** carried **standards** with medals and badges on them, but they also introduced the world's first true flag, called a vexillum. This was a

A Roman flag, or vexillum, could be long or short. Sometimes the material was pleated

square piece of fabric hung from a bar on a long pole. The flag had a picture or some writing on it. The ancient Chinese used many different shaped flags including fans and streamers. These were very colourful but rarely carried a symbol or a picture. The Chinese were also the first to hang flags from one side of a vertical, or upright pole.

Flags at sea

Flags have been particularly important at sea, and are still used to this day. All ships should display the flag of the country where they were registered. Merchant ships carry goods to ports all over the world. Those registered in the UK have the same design with a red background, while a blue background shows that the ship is on government business. However, all American ships, whether merchant or US Navy vessels, fly the Stars and Stripes, which is the flag of the United States.

This is a soldier from a peacetime task force. He is carrying the flag of his **regiment**.

Ships in foreign ports often fly the flag of the country they are visiting, to show respect. When ships are about to leave port, most will fly the Blue Peter. This is a blue flag with a white square in the middle. A yellow flag is flown if the crew are suffering from certain illnesses. It means that the ship is in quarantine and nobody must go aboard.

Long ago, ships flew a wide range of different coloured flags, especially when they went into battle. In the 16th century, the ships of King Henry the Eighth of England were decorated with flags. His most important ship, known as the flagship, was covered with streaming multicoloured flags and the flags of his royal family, the House of Tudor. Many of these flags were used for signalling, or sending messages, because it was difficult to communicate at sea. Signal flags were not invented by King Henry's sailors, but had been used in this way since the time of the Greek and Persian wars of 500 **BC**.

Signal flags were first used to order the captains of the fleet to go to the admiral's ship. Later, each flag came to have a different meaning. By **hoisting** a series of flags in a particular way, a complicated message could be sent to another ship or to the shore. The position of the flag on the flag-pole was an important part of the signal.

Boats in a marina. Can you tell which countries these boats come from by looking at the flags?

Semaphore flags are moved to different positions for each letter of the alphabet. In these photographs the boy is signalling the word STOP

This is the letter **S**

This is the letter **T**

This is the letter **O**

This is the letter **P**

A world peace march in New York. What information can you obtain from the flag, or banner, in the foreground?

Each flag had a different colour and shape to represent a certain word, letter or number. A flag could have more than one meaning depending on whether it was used with other flags or on its own. A red and yellow flag meant the letter 'O' when it was used with other flags. But when it was used on its own it meant 'man overboard'.

Using flags was a very important way of communicating during naval battles. In the Battle of Trafalgar in 1805, Admiral Lord Nelson was able to move his ships into good battle positions by using flag signals.

Another system of communication using flags is called semaphore. The messenger holds a pair of flags, one in each hand, and changes the position of his arms to represent different letters and numbers. These flags are usually a simple bright colour such as red, because the colour is used to make the flag positions easy to see.

Flags as symbols

Flags also carry ideas and messages in their colour and design. Colours and shapes can have symbolic meaning. Traditionally, red stood for courage, royalty and power. More recently, red communist flags have stood for the power of ordinary people, not leaders. White and blue, the

Red Cross and Red Crescent symbols are usually shown on flags and ambulances. Here these symbols have been used on the organizations' exhibition stand at EXPO '92 in Seville, Spain

colours of peace, are found in the flag of the United Nations. Green, the colour of plants and the land, is often used to mean youth and hope.

The shape of the cross is a widely recognized symbol. A red cross on a white background is the symbol of the Red Cross. This organization was **founded** in Switzerland. The founder used the Swiss flag, which is a white cross on a red background, but reversed the colours to produce a red cross on a white background. The Red Cross is an international organization that helps the victims of wars and disasters. The Red Cross does not support any side in a war but remains neutral, helping people of all nationalities. During the First and Second World Wars, the Red Cross helped prisoners of war. Members of the organization visited prison camps and sent out food and clothes parcels, and letters from the prisoners' families.

In some parts of the world, in Muslim countries and among Muslim communities, the cross is replaced by a crescent shape, which is an important religious symbol in Islam. The Muslim organization is actually called the Red Crescent and it helps people in exactly the same way as the Red Cross.

In times of war, white flags have the same meaning all over the world. When one of the sides which is fighting raises a white flag, it shows that it wishes to negotiate, and possibly surrender, or give up fighting. A white flag flown in this way is called a flag of truce.

A flag that is flown at half-mast, that is, halfway up the flag-pole, shows that an important person has died. At the funeral, the flag of the person's country is often draped over the coffin.

Beach signals in Cyprus. The red flag has been hoisted to show danger

21

Above: The chequered flag shows the end of a motorbike race
Right: This EC flag shows that the sea-water is clean

Bright red flags are often used to warn people of danger. A red flag flying on a beach is a warning that the seas are too rough for swimming. It could also mean that there are dangerous currents that might carry a swimmer far out to sea. There are often other flags flying on a beach. Some European beaches fly a blue flag. This tells people that the water is known to be clean and safe for swimming.

Coloured flags can also be used for other purposes, such as marking routes, or simply to attract attention. A football pitch is marked with corner flags, and the linesmen wave brightly coloured flags to attract the attention of the referee. A **chequered** flag is used in motor racing to indicate the end of the race, while a black one means that the driver must retire from the race.

International flags flying together

National flags

For many centuries, since the earliest flags were invented, coloured flags have been used to identify peoples or nations. In the opening ceremony of the Olympic games, all the teams enter the sports arena parading behind their national flags. The Olympic flag is made up of five interlocking coloured rings on a white background. This symbolizes the five continents of the world joined together through sport and friendship (see title page).

The flags of each country are usually easy to recognize, and each has a story to tell. The Danish flag has a red background with a large white cross and is the oldest national flag. It has been flying for 600 years. The Christian symbol of the cross was often used on European flags.

The flag of the United States still bears the colours of the British flag. The United States was once ruled by Britain; it was a colony. In the 18th century, American leaders formed the Continental Congress, which aimed to throw out the British colonial government. But the Congress still wanted to keep the colours of the British flag. At one of their meetings the colours of the American flag were given their symbolic meaning for the rebels: 'White signifies Purity and Innocence; Red, Hardiness and Valour; Blue signifies Vigilance, Perseverance and Justice.'

Not all colonies kept the flag colours of their masters after they gained independence. Many of the new African and Caribbean states used some, or all, of the Pan African colours: black, red, green and gold (see page 38). These symbolize the struggle of black people against their white colonial rulers; red was used to show the blood sacrificed to gain freedom. Other new nations, such as Nigeria, chose green, a colour that reflected the natural wealth of the country. Nigeria felt that her future lay in developing the country's agriculture, so she picked the colour of plants and new life.

Left: The Danish flag
Centre: The Ghanaian flag with the Black Star of Africa
Right: The Stars and Stripes of America

legions: groups of 3000 to 6000 men in a Roman army

standard: a large flag on a flag-pole

allegiance: obedience and loyalty

regiment: a large group of soldiers, commanded by a colonel

BC: the years before the birth of Christ

hoisting: lifting up

founded: created

chequered: marked like a chessboard

COLOURFUL THINGS TO DO!

Each country of the world has its own flag. You should find a selection of them in a stamp album or in an atlas. Flags use patterns of crosses and lines in bright colours, as well as symbols that mean a lot to the country. For example, the maple leaf is the symbol of Canada, the home of the beautiful maple tree. Try to design your own flag. Use bright colours, and symbols that are important to you.

Colours for identification

Colour can be used to show where people work, or the kinds of jobs that they do. It can tell you where a product was made, and it can help you to pick out the exact product that you need. Colour also helps to show ownership. You might put a yellow sticker on all your books so that you can tell they belong to you. So colour can help to identify people, jobs, goods and many other things.

Uniform colours

If you go to school or belong to an organization such as the scouts or girl guides, you might wear a uniform which comes in a particular colour and style.

Many people wear a uniform, although they may not realize they are doing so. If it is the fashion to wear blue denim jeans with trainers and baggy sweat shirts, then a lot of people will follow it. The individual design of the jeans, shoes and tops may be different, but the overall look is the same. People also tend to wear the 'in' colours, as every year clothes' designers try to get us to wear certain colours.

These children at a school near Peking are wearing a bright red uniform. But many school uniforms are made in dark, practical colours which do not show the dirt very quickly

Uniforms are not only found among young people. Many other groups of people, such as bus conductors, nurses, policemen and mechanics, wear a uniform. The colour and style of the uniform are easy to identify, to help us tell what jobs the people do. Clothing is often designed to help people carry out their jobs, to give them an air of authority, and to help them identify with one another as a team. Some groups use different coloured uniforms within their organizations. In Spain, local police wear dark blue and national police wear khaki. In the northern Basque region, the police are distinguished by their bright red berets.

Companies or organizations choose **logos** in colours that are easy to identify. They hope that the colours will become well known and associated with the company – to form a company identity.

Above: A train driver in uniform in Peking. The train guards and station porters usually wear a similar uniform

Colour in goods and services

When we go shopping, we can often recognize and choose goods by the colour of their packaging. Milk cartons and bottles can have different coloured boxes or tops to show how much fat each type of milk contains. Bags of plain and self-raising flour have different coloured lettering. Each company that produces goods such as these uses a different colour scheme. But we learn to recognize the colours they use. We can then choose the exact item that we need.

Colour is used in manufacturing industry to identify the type and quality of raw materials. Different kinds of steel tubing are colour coded so that the right type can be chosen to make specific goods.

Colour can also be used to identify a service, even if it is operated by different companies. It is easy to identify a taxi in New York because all the taxis are bright yellow, making

Above: A green cross identifies this chemist's shop in Normandy, France
Right: Yellow taxis in New York

them easy to spot amongst the traffic. In Indonesia there are *becaks*. These are tri-shaws, or three-wheeled motorized bikes. They are used as taxis and are usually painted in bright colours so that customers can see them easily in the crowded streets of busy cities, such as Jakarta (see page 6).

Trains carry a lot of information. The national railway service of Portugal has green trains. Their first class carriages have a yellow stripe along the side. There may be a blue sign with a number 1 or 2 painted on it. These signs indicate the class of a carriage. Red and white no smoking signs are stuck on the windows. Doors are often painted in a bright colour that is easy to spot in an emergency. The ends of the carriages are sometimes painted in bright colours such as yellow and black diagonal stripes, so that train drivers can see the back of any train in front of them.

Postboxes are usually easy to see as well. In Portugal they are painted bright red, whereas in Germany they are yellow.

A railway carriage in Portugal. What class carriage is it? Can you see any warning colours? Why have they been used?

Colour in sport

Colours for identification are important in sport. The players on a pitch need to be clearly identifiable so that team members can play well together. Each team wears a coloured uniform that is quite different from those of the opposition. The referee usually wears different colours, perhaps black and white, so that he or she can also be easily picked out on the field.

Horse-racing jockeys wear brightly coloured shirts and caps made of silk. They identify the owner of the horse that they are riding. Racegoers must be able to see the colours during the race so they can tell whether the horse is running well or badly. Many spectators at football or rugby matches wear the colours of the team they are supporting. They wear scarves, hats, T-shirts, sweatshirts and rosettes, in their teams' colours.

In the USA, supporters of American football teams make football matches very colourful events. Cheerleaders line the sides of the pitch. They wear the colours of their team and carry huge pompoms and streamers of coloured material. Some people wear elaborate fancy dress for the occasion. Supporters of the Washington Redskins wear complete Indian Chief outfits, including war paint and huge head dresses.

The number identifies the horse. But the jockey's coloured shirt and cap identifies the owner and the racing stable to which the horse belongs

Scottish dancers wearing tartan kilts

National dress

Many people wear a national dress in special colours for celebrations and festivals. In Scotland, the national dress is the kilt. This is a pleated wrap of patterned cloth that reaches down to the knees. The pattern of colours on the kilt is called a tartan. Tartans are in different colours, for each identifies a group of people called a clan.

Two birdwatchers are camouflaged in the grass. The disruptive colour patterns on their shirts act like a zebra's stripes or a leopard's spots against their natural background

Colours for camouflage

Although colours are usually chosen to make things easy to see, there are times when it is better for them to stay hidden. On such occasions, colours can be chosen carefully to help the object blend in with its background. This is known as camouflage. Disruptive colour patterns are often used to help break up the shape of an object so that it cannot be seen easily.

Colour and chemistry

Colour is very important to scientists. It helps them to identify different substances. Chemicals called indicators are often used. Indicators identify certain substances or what they contain. They do this by changing colour when each of the substances is added to them.

Indicators are also very useful when a scientist is trying to work out whether a substance is acid, alkali or neutral. Neutral means that the substance is neither acid nor alkali. The colour of the indicator also shows the strength of the acid or alkali in the substance.

Doctors often use colour to help them find out whether there is anything wrong with their patients. Sometimes people have kidneys that do not work properly. Doctors can carry out two simple tests on urine to help them find out what is the matter. They can test for the presence of glucose, a type of sugar, and for protein, both of which should not normally be in urine. To test for glucose, the doctor takes a strip of plastic about 5 cm long with a blue, chemically treated square at one end. The doctor dips the blue end in the urine. If there is any glucose present it will change to green, then red-brown. The colour change shows the amount of glucose present. To test for protein, the doctor

COLOURFUL WORDS!

logos: symbols with a particular meaning

uses a similar strip of plastic. However, in this test, the colour changes from yellow to green and then to blue if protein is present. There is a colour chart so that the doctor can see how much protein is present.

COLOURFUL THINGS TO DO!

A home-made indicator

In this project you will make your own indicator from red cabbage, to find out if some of the substances in your kitchen are acid or alkali. You should get an adult to help you, especially when you use the cooker. You will need a red cabbage, lemon juice, kitchen cleaner, a cutting board, a knife, a saucepan, some water, a sieve, a large jam jar, and several small jam jars.

1 Cut the cabbage into small pieces using the knife and cutting board. Take care with the knife!

2 Put the sliced cabbage into the saucepan and cover it with water. Place the pan on a cooker and bring the water to the boil.

3 Allow the cabbage to simmer for at least 20 minutes. Turn off the heat and let the water cool for one hour.

4 Use the sieve to strain the water from the cabbage into your large jar. This cabbage water is your indicator.

5 Pour a little of the indicator into a small jam jar and then add a few drops of lemon juice. The colour should change to red, because the lemon is acidic. Make a note of this.

6 Now repeat using fresh indicator and add some drops of water. Water is neutral, which means that it is neither acid nor alkali, so there is no colour change. Make a note of this.

7 Now use some more indicator and add a little kitchen cleaner. Kitchen cleaners contain ammonia, which is alkali, and they should turn the indicator dark green. Make a note of this as well.

You now know what colours to look for: red for acid, purple for neutral and green for alkali. You can try this out on other substances, such as milk, orange juice, baking powder, washing soda, or milk of magnesia. The indicator will probably show many shades of red, purple and green. This is because each substance that is tested will contain different amounts of acid or alkali.

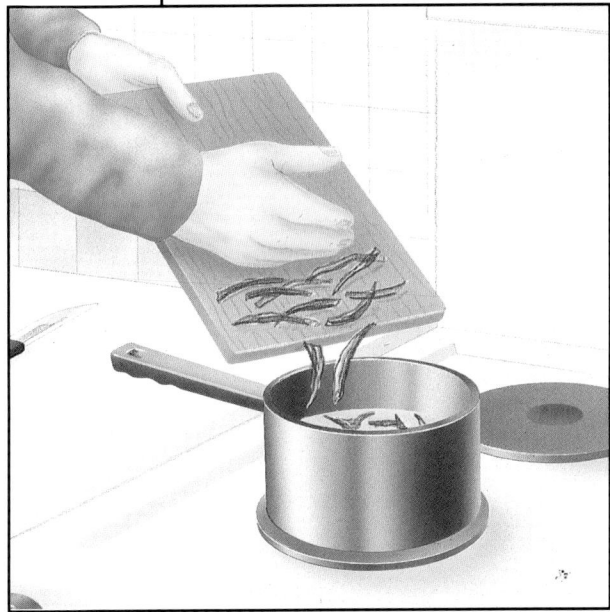

Small pieces of red cabbage are put into a saucepan

Cool cabbage water is strained into a jar. What do the green and red liquids in the small jars indicate?

Colour and body painting

A selection of modern make-up – eye liner, blusher, lipstick and nail varnish

You can learn a lot about people by studying their appearance, which is often a kind of message about themselves. Many people wear make-up, dye their hair, paint their nails, colour their skin, and wear coloured wigs. These colour changes tell us more about people than just their idea of fashion. They can tell us their feelings, their aggressiveness and social position.

Make-up has been used for over 5000 years and has many uses. It can disguise, give protection from the Sun, make us look younger, or show a person's status. The first people to use make-up were the ancient Egyptians. One famous Egyptian queen, Cleopatra, was famous for her make-up. She used coloured eye-shadow on her eyelids, black liner around her eyes, coloured paint on her cheeks and lipstick. But her make-up was not designed just to make her look attractive. It also guarded her face against the strong Egyptian Sun, and repelled flies!

During the 17th century, black beauty spots called patches became very popular. They were used originally to hide marks or scars left by smallpox and other diseases that were very common then.. But they came to have special meaning. You could wear your black spot on the left or right cheek to show your political views.

This wall painting of an Egyptian girl shows her heavy eye make-up. It was found in the ancient Tomb of Menna, Thebes

Above: Face painting in Papua New Guinea
Left: A Plains Indian chief with a painted face pattern and a head-dress made of eagles' feathers (see page 17)

Many Indian tribes of both North and South America paint their faces and bodies. All these tribes have strong links with nature, having lived for hundreds of years in harmony with the environment. Many of the painted patterns are symbols of nature. Natural pigments from plants and the earth are used to paint special body patterns. Red is often used as it stands out against the green leaves of the forest better than any other colour. This is because red and green are complementary colours; they emphasize each other.

North American Indian warriors also painted special patterns on their faces and chests before going into battle with other tribes. These markings were designed to scare the enemy. In many tribes throughout the world the patterns of make-up show the position of a person within the tribe. Some tribes believe that certain patterns of make-up give protection against devils.

The tribesmen of Papua New Guinea are world-famous for their face painting. They produce beautiful, intricate patterns that have been handed down from generation to generation for hundreds of years. The patterns are a form of language, and they are painted following strict rules. Bright patterns can be seen clearly in the dark of the rainforest, where tall trees cut out a lot of light.

Of course, make-up can be easily removed or changed, so the signals it gives are temporary. But people can change their appearance permanently by tattooing their skin. Tattoos mark the skin with colourful patterns, using something sharp to scratch the skin, and dyes to colour it. Sailors sometimes have tattoos on their arms or chests.

Colour associations

Black cats have different associations. They are often thought of as being lucky, but some people associate black cats with evil and bad luck

People associate, or link colours with particular things or events in everyday life. But the use of certain colours often differs from one culture to another. In most of the western world, white is associated with weddings and black with dying. But in India, red is for marriage while white is for death (see pages 39 to 41).

The association of black with fear, death and darkness has led to many expressions that use the word 'black'. For example, a 'blacklist' is a list of names, things or even people, to be avoided. 'Black Magic' refers to dangerous magical powers that cannot be explained. This association of black with death and things that we cannot explain came from a mistake. When ancient Romans changed some Greek words into Latin, they translated the Greek word for 'death' into the Latin word for 'black'!

The meaning of red

Many place names have a colour in them that is linked to their appearance, for example the Black Sea, Greenland and the White Cliffs of Dover. Colours in place names do not always have a colourful meaning. Red Square in Moscow was not named either for the colour of its beautiful red buildings or because it lay in a communist country. The

Red Square in Moscow showing St Basil's Cathedral. St Basil's multi-coloured onion-shaped domes have been compared to turbans or a box of sweets

buildings around Red Square, such as St Basil's Cathedral, are very beautiful and originally the square was called 'Beautiful Square'. It came to be known as Red Square simply because the old Russian word for red was the same as the word for beautiful!

Red is also a famous **revolutionary** colour. It is often associated with communism, particularly in China and the former USSR. Russia first chose red in 1917 to represent its politics. Millions of Russians had been killed or injured during the Russian Revolution of 1917, when ordinary people rose up against their king. The leaders of the people became known as communists. They adopted a blood red banner to represent the blood of the people who died, and with the workers' symbols of the hammer and sickle upon it.

The people of China also overthrew their leader, the Emperor. China became a people's republic in 1949. The Chinese adopted the red flag as well. Their leader, Chairman Mao Tse-Tung, laid down laws for the Chinese. He wrote what is known as the 'little red book', which everybody carried.

The meaning of yellow

Colour has always had strong cultural associations for the Chinese. Before the rise of communism, the ancient Chinese believed that the world was divided into five parts. China

The yellow Yangtze River at the bottom of the Hubei Siling Gorge in China. This very long river eventually flows into the Yellow Sea

33

Yellow ribbon tied to a tree in Dallas, Texas. In America these ribbons serve as a welcome home to soldiers. In 1972, the pop song, "Tie a yellow ribbon round the old oak tree" was a big hit. This song came out at the same time as American soldiers returned home from the Vietnam War.

was thought to be at the centre, so it was called the middle kingdom. The lands to the south were coloured red; those to the north, black; the west, white and the east, blue. The Yellow River, or Yangtze, looks yellow because of the yellow soils over which it runs. It crosses much of China, and early Chinese settlements were built beside the river. So yellow became the most important colour to the Chinese people. It represented power.

Colours have different associations throughout the world. Yellow has a very wide range of meanings and associations. In the East, yellow is a colour of wisdom and is often worn by monks (see page 36). But in the West, it is more often linked with foolishness. In England, yellow has often been associated with being a coward. But in America, yellow ribbons have always had connections with the US army, for the soldiers of the old US cavalry

Yellow is used on this funny costume to attract attention. It also follows a long tradition of being used to make people laugh

had yellow stripes on their trousers and yellow bars on their sleeves.

Going green

Some colours have taken on a **universal** meaning. Green is now a worldwide symbol for the environment. Political parties that want to protect the environment are known as 'The Greens'. There are even 'green' goods in the shops, 'green' issues, and 'green' books. 'Going green' means doing something towards saving the environment. Some companies now use green as their company colour to show that they care about the environment.

Top: A poster advertising the French Green Party during their European Community election campaign
Left: A Greenpeace ship campaigning for a nature park in the waters off Queensland, Australia

COLOURFUL THINGS TO DO!

Colours in names

Colours are used in many place names. Schwarzenberg in Germany means black mountain. Amarillo, a town in the USA, means yellow. In Argentina there is a place called Azul, or blue. On the northern coast of France there is a cape called Gris-Nez, which means grey nose. Use a map to discover the different colours used in place names in your area. The names are often very old and date back several hundreds of years. They often describe the area as it was when the settlement was first built. Can you discover why the colour was used in the name, or what it was supposed to describe or refer to? You may discover that the place names on a map give you a lot of information about the history of an area. Lots of people have colour in their surnames as well. Can you discover why?

COLOURFUL WORDS!

revolutionary: describes wanting a total change

universal: all over the world

Colour in religion

Right: Buddhist priests from Thailand dressed in yellow robes

Below: A Roman Catholic cardinal dressed in red robes

Colours have religious as well as cultural associations. Yellow is the colour of wisdom and **harmony** (see page 34). So Buddhist priests and Hindu monks wear yellow robes to show that they are in harmony with the environment. In the Roman Catholic faith, cardinals, who are leading priests, wear deep red robes. These represent the blood of Christ. The Pope's robes and cap are white, which shows purity.

In the early days of Christianity, in some parts of the Middle East and Mediterranean areas, both Christians and Jews were ordered to wear yellow, to make them stand out from the ruling Muslims. In 1271, King Edward the First of England made all Jews wear a yellow badge above their heart so that they could be identified easily. In Germany during the 1930s and 1940s, Nazi leaders made Jews wear yellow stars, and paint large yellow star shapes on their

These houses in Jodhpur, India, have been painted blue to show that they belong to Hindu Brahmin priests

shops and homes. The sign identified the Jews and made it easy for them to be picked out and **persecuted**.

Colour in Islam

In some parts of the Islamic, or Muslim world, women are required to wear black and cover their bodies with a loose-fitting robe and veil called chador. Muslim men can wear clothes of any colour, although they often wear white. Every Muslim has to try to make a pilgrimage to the holy city of Mecca, in Saudi Arabia, at least once in their lives. When pilgrims are 9 km away from the holy city, the men have to wash and dress themselves in two white, unsewn towels before going on to the Great Mosque. The white towels symbolize purity and simplicity.

Muslim children wearing their brightest clothes for a festival in Saudi Arabia

Inside the Great Mosque is the sacred Black Stone, or Ka'ba. It is really a dark red colour but is still called black. Pilgrims have to go round the Ka'ba seven times and complete a number of other tasks, some of them outside Mecca, before they return to the Great Mosque. On the final feast day of the pilgrimage, pilgrims take off their white robes and replace them with their brightest clothes.

Rastafarian colours

In Jamaica and many other parts of the world, many people follow the Rastafarian religion. This religion has strong links with four colours: black, red, green and gold. Rastafarianism dates back to the conquest of Jamaica by the English

Rastafarian clothes are on sale in a special shop in Jamaica. Earrings, beads, badges and bags in Rastafarian colours are also sold in a shop like this.

in 1655, when groups of runaway slaves and ex-slaves banded together. Rastafarians believe that all people are equal but that since the arrival of white people in Africa, black Africans have been oppressed, put into slavery and treated poorly. They believe that eventually they will all return to Africa to become one large nation.

The modern Rastafarian religion was started in the early years of this century by a Jamaican called Marcus Garvey. He designed a red, black and green flag, based on the colours of the flag of Ethiopia. Ethiopia was an old name for Africa. The colours are also known as Pan Africanist. Each colour has a special meaning – red is for the spilled blood of black people, green represents nature, and black represents the black skin of Africans. Much later, gold was added to the colours.

Rastafarians wear their hair in long coils, known as dreadlocks, because they believe it is wrong to cut it. They often cover their hair with a tall, peaked cap called a tam. The cap is usually made of wool or corduroy, with ribbons in the Rastafarian colours sewn on to it. Clothes and badges in the Rastafarian colours are also worn. Rastafarian paintings and prayer sticks use the traditional colours.

Colour in marriage

Hundreds of different religious ceremonies take place each day around the world. They may celebrate joyous occasions such as a good harvest, or a wedding. They can also mark someone's death. Wedding ceremonies are particularly important occasions in all cultures. They are usually very colourful and happy events, and in some countries the marriage ceremony can be extremely elaborate.

Main: A Sikh bride and groom at their wedding
Inset: A Hindu bride has her hands beautifully decorated with henna before her wedding

Hindu weddings take a lot of preparation. Before the wedding, the bride bathes and her friends paint complicated patterns on her hands and feet using an orange or black dye called henna. The bride wears a lot of jewellery and a red dress known as a sari. Red is an important colour, for it signifies happiness. A spot of red paste is put on her forehead, and a grain of rice is stuck to the paste. A red spot on the forehead indicates that a woman is married. The groom often wears a

White is the traditional colour for the bride (and sometimes the groom) in Western countries. But many people from other cultures now wear it as well

long white tunic and trousers. He might wear a red turban on his head.

Similar traditions are followed by Sikh brides, who also wear red clothes. These are either a sari, or a tunic and trousers called shalwar and khameez. The bride and groom often wear garlands of flowers around their necks, and each carries a long scarf, again usually red. The scarves are tied together during the ceremony to show that the man and woman have been joined in marriage.

Deathly colours

Certain colours are associated with death and funerals, just as they are with marriage ceremonies. In Christian and Jewish traditions, the colour worn at funerals is a sombre black. The car that carries the dead body is black as well. It is also a tradition that the letter paper that is used to inform somebody of a death, is edged in black. People often wear black armbands to show respect towards someone who has died. Flowers and wreaths are often sent to the dead person's family as a sign of sympathy and remembrance. White flowers such as arum lilies are traditional funeral flowers.

In many Mediterranean countries, such as Spain and Portugal, mothers who have lost a child, and wives who

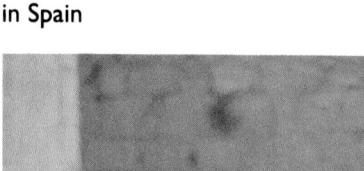

Women in black crossing a bridge in Spain

Left: Flowers being sold for Hindu funerals in Calcutta, India. Orange marigolds are very popular for funerals and are sold in almost every market

Below: In many Western countries arum lilies like these are given at funerals

have lost husbands usually wear black for the rest of their lives. They wear black for several years when they mourn the death of their mother or father. In these countries, it is not uncommon to see most of the older women of a town or village wearing black. However, black was not always worn at funerals. In early Christian times, white was the colour of mourning. It was not until the 5th century that Saint Benedict started to use black for burying his Benedictine monks. By the 11th century, black was used by the rest of European society.

White is still the colour of mourning amongst Hindus and Muslims. A Hindu will pass through 16 stages of life, the last one being cremation, when the body is burnt after death. At a Hindu funeral, the body is draped in a white cloth, covered with many flowers and mounted on a wooden funeral pyre. The wood is then set alight and the body is burnt. Three days later the ashes are collected and scattered on a river. The mourners at the funeral wear white saris.

In China, funerals can be very colourful ceremonies. The Taoist Chinese believe that after death, the soul of the dead person has to cross a bridge to pass into the next life. The body is placed in a coffin and taken to the graveyard. The funeral procession that accompanies the coffin is both colourful and incredibly noisy, for fireworks, drums, dancers and musicians are used to chase away evil spirits. The coffin is decorated in colourful patterns, and red banners are placed near it for good luck. The people attending the funeral all wear white.

COLOURFUL WORDS!

harmony: describes how people or things work together without disturbing or harming each other

persecuted: describes how someone is ill-treated or punished because of their beliefs

Colourful festivals

Not all festivals are religious. There are days to celebrate victory in battle, a country's independence, and hundreds of others. Some of the most colourful ones occur during the dark winter months, when the days are short. Way back in history, people knew that the Sun gave life. They believed that as the days became shorter and the Sun appeared to be losing the struggle against the darkness, they could help the Sun by holding festivals of light, with torchlit processions and bright bonfires.

Colour in the New Year

Many different cultures celebrate the coming of the New Year. One of the most colourful celebrations is the Chinese New Year. The Chinese use the lunar calendar. This is a type of calendar based on the cycle of the moon. Each month is therefore exactly 28 days long. So the Chinese New Year does not fall on 1st January, but between 21st January and 20th February. On New Year's Day there are street carnivals and processions, with the sound of snapping explosions of firecrackers. The highlight of the day comes when a giant coloured paper dragon, operated by many men inside its body, dances frantically through the streets with great swooping movements. The end of the day is marked by a firework display.

Hindus and Sikhs celebrate the festival of Diwali, the Festival of Light, to mark the beginning of the new farming

This colourful flower festival takes place each year in Spalding, England. Magnificent floats made from a variety of flowers parade through the town in celebration of springtime.

Two dragons dance around a town square to celebrate the Chinese New Year. The Chinese often shine red lanterns during festivals because red is a lucky colour

42

Left: A table has been laid for the Diwali festival. Coloured lights surround a shrine
Above: Divas being lit for Diwali

year. The festival is held when the new moon rises in late October or early November, when the nights are very long. Cities, towns and villages glow as candles and small lamps are hung in doors and windows. Public buildings are brightly lit with multicoloured lamps. Some of these lamps, called divas, are made from pottery and give out a lovely golden light. Firework displays often light up the skies.

One of the favourite stories told at this time is the tale of the god, Rama, and his wife, Sita, who returned safely to the village of Ayodhya, guided by the bright lights of Diwali. Since they are celebrating the start of the New Year, many people hold rituals to honour Lakshmi, the goddess of wealth. Homes are cleaned ready for the New Year, and people wear special clothes. Young girls place lamps on tiny rafts and take them to a river, where they allow them to float downstream. It is thought to be good luck if their lamp continues to burn until it is out of sight.

The Goddess Kali

While Diwali is being celebrated, people of Bengal in India also hold a festival to honour Kali, the goddess of strength, disease and death. Bengalis cover their homes with strings of lights and line the streets with **shrines**. Although richer families have very highly decorated shrines, the basic design of all of them is the same. In the middle there is an image of Kali, set against a backdrop of brilliantly coloured cloth and surrounded by flowers and **incense** burners. In the evening, the shrines are lit by oil lamps that give a golden glow. People walk through the streets at night, stopping at shrines to offer gifts in honour of Kali. The night ends with a colourful firework display. Finally, all the images of Kali are taken to the river where they are set afloat to drift downstream.

Carnival colours

Carnivals take place in most countries where Christianity is the main religion. Many of these festivals occur just before Lent, the period before Easter. Lent is a time of fasting, when people are not supposed to eat foods that come from animals for 40 days and 40 nights. The word 'Carnival' means 'to take away meat'. Carnivals were originally held as a final celebration before the fasting started, and as a chance to eat and drink the stores of foodstuffs that would not keep through Lent. Since Lent begins on Ash Wednesday, all carnivals must end the day before, on Shrove Tuesday.

Most carnivals are processions of colourful, highly decorated floats. The annual carnival in Rio is probably the world's largest and certainly the most famous. Planning for the carnival starts as soon as the previous one has finished. The people of Rio form groups called Samba schools. They spend huge amounts of money to make costumes, build

Spectacular costumes in the Rio Carnival in Brazil

floats and practise dancing. These schools try to win prizes that are awarded for the best display and the best dancing. The spectacular costumes and intricate floats are an amazing sight. Processions pass very slowly through the crowded streets until at last they reach the judging area. There is a lot of loud Samba music and dancers move around the floats in fantastic glittering costumes. Floats can often be 10 metres tall and over 10 metres long. Each one carries the queen of the Samba school. She wears the largest and most splendid costume of all. The dancing and music continue day and night for two whole weeks.

The boat race

Dragon-boat festivals are held in China. They are very colourful events that act out an ancient story about a man called Ch'u Yuan. He drowned himself in a lake to protest against the Emperor's cruel treatment of the people. The evil spirits of the lake, and the local people, raced to get to the body first. People distracted the evil spirits by throwing rice cakes into the water while they searched for the body. The boat races are exciting re-enactments of this race.

COLOURFUL WORDS!

shrines: places or objects of worship

incense: perfume

The dragon-boat festival in Hong Kong. The boats have been painted and decorated in bright colours

Index

Further Reading

Flags William Crampton, Eyewitness Guide, (Dorling Kindersley)
Seasonal Festivals: Spring, Summer, Autumn and Winter Mike Rosen, (Wayland)
Religious topics: Birth, Death, Initiation, Pilgrimage, Feasts, Marriage Jon Mayled (Wayland)